T

from **confetti.co.uk**
don't get married without us…

First published in 2004 by Octopus Publishing Group
2–4 Heron Quays, London E14 4JP
www.conran-octopus.co.uk
Reprinted in 2005

ISBN 1 84091 362 2

Publishing Director Lorraine Dickey
Senior Editor Katey Day
Assistant Editor Sybella Marlow
Art Director Chi Lam
Designer Victoria Burley
Assistant Production Controller Natalie Moore

Contents

First things first

From ancient times, brides have been celebrated in poetry and prose as all that is good, pure and beautiful. That's some myth to live up to!

Reality bites

In reality, being a bride-to-be can be very stressful. However natty your fiancé looks in his waistcoat and tails, you know all eyes will be on you as you come down the aisle. And as your parents may be hosting the day, you might also feel responsible for how much money it's costing them, and worry about things going to plan.

Expect the unexpected

Our best advice to you is to relax.
Things will go wrong. Not everything will
turn out exactly as you expected. You'll
have to compromise on some things, for
reasons of cost or practicality, or simply to
avoid someone sulking. And you won't feel
remotely pure, beautiful or good when
you're haggling with your in-laws over
the length of their guest list!

Think ahead

So make sure you look after yourself in the run-up to the wedding. Take your time making important decisions (so start planning well in advance), and allow Confetti to help you. We've got an easy-to-use budget planner and to-do list, plus all the answers to all the wedding questions you can think of. You can even email your personal wedding worries to our online agony aunt at the confetti café.
See www.confetti.co.uk for help.

Planning the big day

What do I need to do?

As well as finding the perfect outfits
and accessories for yourself and your
attendants, you also need to decide who
will be bridesmaids, pageboys and other
attendants, and how you want them to
look. In fact, most of the things that
create those finishing touches are
dependent on the bride's chosen
style and colour scheme.

Who pays for what?

If the wedding is to be paid for by
your parents, then traditionally most
of the arrangements for the invitations,
reception, catering and photography will
be your mother and father's responsibility.
However, modern brides may get involved
in as many aspects of their wedding as
they choose!

Keep the peace
Wherever possible, try to work
hand-in-hand with your parents to
reach joint decisions that you are all happy
with – and make sure you represent the
views of your fiancé in the negotiations
too. There may well be rows, but avoid
the temptation to run off to Gretna
Green: it'll soon pass.

Something to bear in mind...

Decisions about the wedding ceremony itself are for you and your fiancé, and you alone. Apart from the celebrant, no one else should get involved. You can show this page to anyone who disagrees!

Setting the date

It's never too early to decide upon the date for the wedding – the longer you have to prepare, the more likely you are to get exactly what you want, without being rushed into making hasty decisions.

A significant date

When deciding on a date for your wedding, you'll need to think about when the best man, bridesmaids and ushers are free to attend, not forgetting important relatives and close friends. You might want your wedding date to be one of special significance. You might also want to calculate a date that does not coincide with your period!

Choosing your attendants

There's no rule that says you have to have attendants, but if you do, choose carefully! Your bridesmaids should be there to lend you support and help, and not to add to your stress. So don't choose anyone who already has their hands full with a new job or a new baby. Remember, too, that it's your wedding, not your bridesmaids'. So while they will be excited for you, don't expect them to drop everything else in their lives!

Chief bridesman?

What if your best friend or the only person whose taste you trust or your favourite shopping partner is actually a man? No worries. There's an increasing trend for bridal attendants to be of either gender. Just be sure to clear it with your fiancé – otherwise he may be a little surprised to find another man at the altar!

Give it to them straight

When inviting people to be your attendants, always make it clear who will pay for their outfits. If there is to be a substantial financial outlay involved, it's best to clarify this at the outset to avoid upset later. This is particularly important where small children are involved: always check first with her parents before you promise little Tessa she can be a bridesmaid!

Help! I've got too many bridesmaids!
So, in the first flush of excitement, you invited your whole address book to be your bridesmaids? Don't worry. Other ways to get people involved in your wedding include giving readings or performing songs at the ceremony, assisting with the guest book or acting as toastmaster or mistress at the reception.

Planning the ceremony

Once the wedding date is set, you and your groom should contact the minister or celebrant of the church in which you wish to be married. If the wedding is to take place in a register office or civil venue, visit the superintendent registrar for your area.

How much will it cost?

There's only one real rule when it comes to budgeting for your wedding: limit your plans to the type of wedding you can realistically afford.

How much?

According to Confetti users, it seems that
the average wedding costs about £15,300.
This includes around £1,200 for the rings,
£1,400 for the wedding outfits and
essential pampering in the run-up to the
big day and £1,300 for the wedding itself.
The reception adds a further £3,500, and
then, of course, there's the honeymoon and
other expenses that vary from
couple to couple.

Decide who's paying for what

Traditionally, it falls to the father of the bride to pick up the tab for the main event, with the groom chipping in for the church or registry fees and the all-important honeymoon. But more and more couples now choose to pay for the bulk of their wedding themselves.

Early planning pays off

It's important to work out from the start
who is paying for what and whether there
are any financial constraints. For example,
is the bride's father willing to pay for the
horse and carriage to the church? And how
many guests can you afford to invite to
the main reception?

Stick to your budget

Confetti's interactive budget planner, which gives the average costs normally paid out for a wedding, can get you started on calculating how much to spend on each item. Whether it's your money or your parents' purse that's paying, it's essential to set a limit.

Contingency plan

Planning your wedding is stressful enough
without arguments erupting over the costs.
Allow a further ten per cent on top of your
budget to cope with the inevitable extras.

Shop around

The easiest way to save money is not
to pay over the odds. So shop around for
your venue, dress, photographer and so on.
Ask for quotations in writing, and make
sure you know exactly what the agreed
price covers. Remember, you may need to
add VAT to some prices, so always ask.

Cut down on costs

- Consider a weekday wedding when venues generally charge less.
- Check if you can supply your own Champagne and wine. Hop across the Channel, where it costs considerably less.
- Hire your wedding dress or, if you're handy at sewing, make your own.
- Ask your mum or her friends to do the church flowers and save on florist's fees.

Cut down on costs

- Use a good photographer, but preferably one whose company is small enough not to charge VAT (saving you 17.5%).
- Make use of friends with posh cars to ferry wedding guests to the church.
- Invite more casual friends to an evening drink rather than the full wedding with all its catering costs.

Cut down on costs

- Ask a relative or friend with culinary talents to make the cake as their wedding gift to you.
- You may even decide to ask guests to chip in for your celebration, although for many people this is a contentious issue. Some couples get round this by having an informal reception (usually the biggest chunk of wedding expense) and asking guests to bring a specific dish, or contribute to a buffet.

29

Take out cover

As a last word, wedding insurance is worth considering. This will cover you in the event of damage to your dress, theft of presents, cancellation of the reception (e.g. because of illness), double-booking of the venue, and so on. Policies cost around £50 to £100, but bear in mind they don't cover you against getting cold feet on your big day!

PLANNING THE BIG DAY

The reception

The bride's family is usually responsible for making all the arrangements and absorbing the cost, which can mean shelling out for food, drink, a wedding cake, caterers, waiting staff, a toastmaster, flower arrangements, a band or disco, entertainers or musicians and any security arrangements. Sometimes couples cover the cost of the wedding reception themselves, or share it between the families. Whoever's paying, the wedding reception is likely to be the single biggest expense of the wedding, so plan it carefully.

31

The early bird catches the worm

Planning for your reception should begin as soon as you set the wedding date. Popular venues (or any venue on popular dates such as a bank holiday) may need to be reserved up to a year before the event, so make a provisional booking as soon as you can.

10 or 100?

The number of people you want at your reception may well dictate your choice of venue – or vice versa! It is usual for everyone who has been invited to the wedding ceremony to be asked to the reception. If only a small number of guests can attend the ceremony owing to lack of space, or you want a very private ceremony, then additional guests can be invited to the reception afterwards.

Working out the costs

For 100 guests or more, consider rooms
designed specifically for holding receptions,
as they will have all the facilities you need.
Most reception venues will quote you a
cost per head for food and drink, plus
a hire charge for the venue (or hire of a
marquee), plus the cost of any entertainment,
a toastmaster, cake stand, etc.

Making sense of it all

In your initial consultation with a
venue, get a full list of all the possible
costs and charges. Decide roughly what
your budget is and your ideal head count,
and then the venue price range will
become clear. If you register for the
handy 'my confetti' service, you'll have
access to a free budget planner.

Is it what you really want?

Once you've got a particular venue in mind, there are some important questions to ask to make sure that it really is suitable for the sort of reception you want:

- Are there adequate cloakroom and lavatory facilities?
- Are there facilities for less mobile guests or anyone with a disability?
- Are there sufficient car-parking spaces?

Is it what you really want?

- Is the reception venue within a reasonable distance of the ceremony? Is it easy to find or well signposted?
- Will the reception venue allow you to have the kind of reception you've planned? Check carefully for things such as licensing laws and late-night curfews.
- Is there accommodation at the venue or nearby for out-of-town guests?
- Are decorations included, or will you have to provide your own balloons, flowers and table decorations?

Invitations and stationery

The first job is to decide on the guest list, and this is usually where the wedding party comes to blows. While invitations are traditionally sent out by the bride's parents, the bride and groom should have the chance to invite a similar number of guests. One way is to split the list into thirds – one third for your family, one third for your fiancés family and one third for your friends.

Get tough

Start by asking everyone involved to make a rough list, then start pruning! Ultimately, whoever is paying for the wedding should have the final say on numbers, but really the hosts and couple should have the final say on who makes the cut!

Don't forget...

You should add the names of the minister and his or her partner to your list as a matter of courtesy. And when it comes to working out numbers, make sure you include all members of the wedding party – people sometimes forget to add themselves!

On the list

If you have relatives or friends whom you know won't be able to make it on the day, you obviously don't need to include them on your guest list, but make sure you send them an invitation anyway. Many people, in particular very elderly relatives, really appreciate this gesture — it shows that you haven't just forgotten or ignored them.

Setting the scene

The design of the invitations can set the style and tone you wish to create for your wedding, be it traditional or out of the ordinary. And it's not just the invitations you can customize: save-the-date cards, reply cards, the order of service, menus, place cards and thank-you cards can all be coordinated, and it's best to order them all at least three months in advance. Check www.confetti.co.uk/invitations for a wide range of co-ordinating stationery in many styles.

Wording

The wording may vary according to taste but, whatever the format, the invitation should state the following:

- names of the bride's parents or other hosts
- first name of the bride
- first name and surname of the bridegroom and his title (Mr/Lieutenant/Sir)
- where the ceremony is taking place
- date, month and year of the ceremony
- time of the ceremony
- location of the wedding reception
- address to which guests should reply

Information packs

This is where you can include maps, your gift list details, information about accommodation and anything else your guests need to know. More sensitive messages, such as 'We are sorry, but we are unable to accommodate children', should be included here and not printed on the invitation.

For more details on all aspects of invitations and other stationery, see www.confetti.co.uk or the Confetti book *Wedding and Special Occasion Stationery*.

The gift list

Most guests welcome advice on what to
buy, so make your list as comprehensive
and wide-ranging as possible to cover a
price range for all pockets. When drawing
up the list, be specific about what make,
model and colour of item you want.
Try to list many more items than you have
guests, so that no one is left having to buy
the Mickey Mouse salt cellar. Make sure
you state how many of each item you
want: matching towels don't match if
you have only one!

Gift-list etiquette

What you put on your gift list will depend on your stage of life. Younger couples may be in need of the basics, whereas brides starting a second marriage will usually already have all the household items they need. So don't be afraid of having an alternative list, such as a wine cellar or book list – the idea of a gift list is to give you something to help you start married life together, and if you don't need a garlic crusher, there's no point in asking for one!

Asking for money

Many modern couples would like something big on their list, such as a new bathroom or three-piece suite – but few of us know anyone rich or generous enough to buy one as a gift! So why not ask guests to contribute towards a larger gift by donating to the 'Bride and Groom Sofa Fund'? Make sure you invite everyone round to sit on it once you've bought it!

Cue music

Without music, as the Spanish say, life would be a mistake – and for many people music plays an equally important part at weddings. Including your favourite pieces is the easiest way to personalize the ceremony, as well as setting the style and mood, adding dignity to your vows and creating a memorable day for everyone involved.

Raising the rafters

If you're hoping for some hearty singing, take into account how many guests are coming and their likely familiarity with the songs or hymns you've chosen. For more intimate occasions, instrumental music and a group or choir leading the sung pieces may be more appropriate. If all or part of your ceremony is taking place outside, make sure you choose rousing pieces that will carry, or that there is good amplification.

Music in register office ceremonies

A register office ceremony must not contain religious music or readings, nor any music that might detract from the solemnity of the occasion.

Register office ceremonies are generally shorter than religious ceremonies, leaving fewer opportunities for music. You may want some recorded music playing while people arrive/depart or the register is signed, but check your choice of music with the registrar well in advance.

Readings loud and clear

Readings can add to the solemnity of an occasion or provide a welcome moment of light relief. In civil weddings, they may add colour and individuality to the formulaic; in religious venues, they can provide a breath of worldliness that non-religious people can relate to. Above all, readings underline the importance of your day by articulating the deep values underlying your momentous decision to marry.

Church weddings

For a religious ceremony, you are usually given a selection of biblical readings, but you may have the option of secular texts. This depends on the church and the minister; a High Anglican vicar, for instance, might allow Shakespeare but draw the line at modern poetry, whereas a 'trendy vicar' might consider a wider selection of texts. Both, however, would want to ensure that the readings do not undermine the Christian view of marriage, so make sure your choice is approved by the minister or celebrant.

Register office

At a register office wedding, you don't
need to have any readings and you must
obtain prior approval to use any. Similarly,
in weddings that take place in state-
licensed venues, a registrar will need to
approve your choice of readings.
Remember, too, that civil weddings do
not allow for any material with a religious
content or any references to religion.
Obviously this rules out biblical texts
and hymns, but also more loosely
spiritual material.

Who reads the readings?

Generally, you and your fiancé get to choose who gives the readings on the day. This is often a useful way of including in your ceremony a close friend or relative whom you didn't have room for as an usher/bridesmaid, or who lives too far away to be able to be more involved in the preparations.

There are a number of books on readings in this series, and you can find out more about choosing your readings at www.confetti.co.uk

Flower power

There are really only three rules when it comes to organizing the flowers for your wedding: plan well in advance, choose the varieties you like to complement the style of your day and use someone who knows what they're doing.

Blooming marvellous

Flowers will usually be needed in the ceremony venue as centrepieces on reception tables, in the bride's and bridesmaids' bouquets and as buttonholes and corsages. They could also be used in the bride's headdress or to adorn the cake. The bride's flowers set the tone and scheme for all the other floral arrangements.

The bouquet

There are many different types of bridal bouquet, from a wild flower posy to a basket of flowers, and from a single amazing stem of lilies to a traditional sheaf of varied blooms. Some brides choose a silk bouquet, which lasts forever. There are many companies who will preserve your fresh flower bouquet, too.

Picture perfect

You can't repeat this day, so it's essential that you find and invest in a good, reliable photographer. Start your search early, as good photographers get booked up. Try to visit at least three photographers. Ask to see full wedding album samples and make sure that the photographs are the work of the photographer who will be taking your wedding pictures – not simply the best photos from the studio.

Capturing the cost

Most photographers have a menu of prices and will charge you a flat rate for taking shots on the day, plus an additional charge based on how many photographs you want in your album. The quality of the albums on offer (leather, plastic, velvet) can vary and this affects the cost, too. Remember that your family will be charged separately for any copies they want. Look for those little extras though – some throw in thank-you cards with a small photo as part of the deal.

Photo style

There are lots of ways for your photographer to record your wedding, from the traditional posed group shots in colour to more candid reportage-style shots, such as you in your curlers. Most couples go for a combination of styles.

For more informal snaps, it's a lovely idea to place single-use cameras on the tables at the reception so your guests can capture their version of the day.

Transport

The transport is usually the groom's responsibility, but here are some key things to consider. When hiring a car, make sure you see it before booking or paying a deposit – photos and leaflets don't show marks, dents or a scruffy interior. Also, the wedding car will be the backdrop for several wedding photos, so make sure the colour doesn't clash with your bouquet or the bridesmaids' dresses.

A decorative touch

Buy the ribbon for the front of the car well in advance and ask a reliable (and handy) member of the bridal party to attach it to the car on the day. This can be surprisingly fiddly and, for a professional result, practice is essential.

In the excitement of booking your car, don't forget the other members of the bridal party. You will also need transport for your mum and the bridesmaids.

Do yourself a favour

Favours (or bomboniere) are little gifts given to each guest at a wedding. They are integrated into the colour theme and are often placed at each guest's seat as a token of thanks. They can be personalized to the event, long-lasting and elegant, or a simple, edible treat!

Traditional vs modern

Traditional wedding favours are sugared almonds, also known as 'confetti almonds'. Five are given, representing health, happiness, fertility, long life and wealth. But there are many different versions now, so if almonds aren't your thing, don't despair. Look at www.confetti.co.uk/shopping for inspiration.

Confetti

Confetti is the ultimate symbol of weddings and has come a long way since the days when sugar-coated grain and nuts were thrown over newlyweds. Nowadays, as well as the paper form we all know, it is available in all kinds of materials and is used for decorating tables, strewing on paths and including in invitations, as well as for throwing.

Confetti

Many venues today will not allow the throwing of paper confetti. A good alternative is to use confetti made of real flower petals, but if even that's forbidden, then bubbles are a great option – they even show up well in photographs.

Hen nights

Strictly speaking, the hen night is the responsibility of the chief bridesmaid. So choose her well! Make sure you've discussed what kind of event you want to have beforehand. Nowadays the 'last night of freedom' is often a weekend or longer!

Inspiring ideas

Favourite hen activities include pampering sessions: if you can't afford a trip to a spa, then ask all the hens to bring face masks, foot baths and nail polish and do it yourselves. Activity hen nights, involving such activities as pottery or line dancing, are also popular. Or why not enter the territory of the stag and try paintballing or tank driving?

Hags and stens

Joint hen and stag parties are increasingly popular with modern couples, who often have many mutual friends. Book a private room at a smart restaurant, or even take over a cottage in the country for the weekend, and party!

Bridal beauty

Choosing the dress

Although you've probably got lots of ideas
and may well have been dreaming of the
perfect dress for months or even years, it's
best to seek out some professional advice
to make sure that the final creation fits and
flatters you perfectly, too – accentuating
your good points and minimizing the rest.

Reverse angle

Whatever style you decide on, it's worth remembering that for most ceremonies, the back view is as important as the front as the guests will be behind you. It's a good idea to choose a fabric that's resistant to crushing and creasing. If you want to have a train, it's wise to make it detachable so that it can be removed (or hooked up) at the reception for dancing.

Coordination

It may be a good idea to discuss your
ideas with the groom to ensure that the
colour and style of your dress will
complement his outfit and all the attendants'.
There is no need to reveal the finer details
of the dress, as traditionally these should
not be known by the groom until he sees
his bride, looking gorgeous, walking down
the aisle towards him.

Colour inspiration

Wearing white for a wedding is a symbol of purity and first became popular in the 18th century. But if white does not suit your complexion or tastes, why not dress in your favourite colour? Wedding gowns in cream, pale gold, pale blue and pink are all quite usual now, and there's been a recent move to much deeper colours in shades of green or even burgundy – particularly stunning for a winter wedding.

Decisions, decisions

When buying your dress, take someone along with you whose opinions and judgment you trust, as it's a big decision to make alone. It is best to try on as many different styles as you can and view them from all angles.

Specialist bridal departments and shops keep dozens of styles in a range of sizes, and most provide a fitting and alteration service at extra cost. You may need to book an appointment in some of the more popular shops.

THE BRIDE'S WEDDING

Your accessories

Accessories may include shoes, jewellery,
gloves, a veil and tiara and underwear. You
should always wear your wedding shoes
and underwear to your fittings, to make
sure the dress is the right length and fits
in all the right places.

Bridal beauty

There are two rules to looking good on your wedding day: start early and stick at it!

The larger department stores often offer free beauty consultations especially for brides-to-be. This is a good place to start. Discuss any skin problems and find out which of the good-quality skin-care preparations will suit your skin. Regular cleansing, toning and moisturizing will keep you blemish-free and looking healthy.

Make-up

If you opt to do your own make-up
on the day, make sure you buy any new
cosmetics early on and practise with them.
When you're trying out make-up, it's
important to wear something the same
colour as your wedding dress, or take with
you a piece of material in the same colour
that you can drape to get the same effect.

Leave it to the professionals

If you fancy a new look for the wedding, something more glamorous perhaps, a make-up lesson from a beauty salon is a great way to pick up a few new ideas and techniques. Alternatively, if you think your hands will be shaking too much on the big day, or you just like the idea of some last-minute pampering, book a beautician to come to the house. Just make sure you fit in a practice session beforehand.

Handle with care

Don't forget that your hands will become the focus of attention when showing off your newly acquired wedding ring. So be careful to avoid doing anything that will cause nails to split and break, and take extra care when shaping them. Use loads of hand cream in the weeks leading up to the great day to get them super soft and smooth, and the day before the wedding have a professional manicure.

To diet or not to diet?

You may have decided to lose a few pounds
before your wedding day, but don't set
yourself unrealistic targets. It's difficult to
stick to a diet at the best of times, and
when you're stressed out it's even harder.
Chances are you'll lose weight anyway,
rushing around doing all that organizing.

Wedding hair

Make an appointment with your
hairdresser well in advance to discuss your
wedding day hairstyle, especially if you are
planning something a bit different. Book
some practice sessions and take along
your headdress and veil.

Have a good hair day

Remember, good hairdressers tend to
get booked up early, particularly on
Saturdays and during the summer holidays.
If you decide to do your own hair, practise
fixing the headdress (and taking it off)
before the actual day.

Pre-wedding nerves

Don't worry!

At some point, you might wonder if you're doing the right thing by getting married at all. This can be a very scary feeling, especially if money has begun to be spent and you feel that everyone has great expectations for you and your partner.

Keep a cool head

But remember, most people have wobbly moments as their wedding approaches. Getting married is a big deal. It's meant to be forever and, as the song goes, that's a mighty long time. Frankly, you should probably worry more if you're not scared!

On a serious note...

As a rule of thumb, it's only if these misgivings last for several weeks that you need to consider seriously if you're doing the right thing. Take a deep breath and tell your partner how you feel. Consider putting the wedding date back to give you both time to resolve any issues with other major life events, such as moving house or bereavement.

Eat to beat the stress

Feelings of stress and bad moods can be exacerbated if you don't make a point of looking after yourself, now of all times. Make sure you eat a balanced diet, rich in wholefoods and fresh fruit and veg (aim for five portions a day). Bananas, green leafy veg, fish and oats are all natural stress-busters. Cut down on salt, sugar and refined stuff, and don't overdo stimulants such as tea, coffee and alcohol.

Exercise away your stress

Hundreds of studies have shown exercise to be a significant stress-buster and mood-enhancer. Frequent aerobic activity raises your fitness and energy levels, relaxes tense muscles and helps trigger 'feel-good' chemicals in the brain known as endorphins. Aim to work out three times a week, choosing activities that leave you out of breath. Include stuff you enjoy, such as dancing or swimming.

Sleep like a baby

A poor sleep pattern is a strong stress trigger, leading to irritability, nerves and even temporarily reduced IQ! Aim to be in bed before midnight and/or try to get eight hours sleep a night. Tuck yourself up before you actually need to fall asleep, so you have an unwinding period when you can listen to gentle music or read.

Natural remedies

A number of natural remedies are
thought to help alleviate stress. Take a
look in your local health-food shop.
For sudden feelings of panic and anxiety,
many stars swear by Rescue Remedy, a
homeopathic flower tincture. Just put
a few drops on your tongue
whenever you feel the need.

Learn to delegate

Feeling responsibility for every aspect of your wedding can be a hugely stressful burden. Spend as much time as possible planning what needs to be done – but also who is going to do it. You're likely to be surrounded by offers of help, so don't turn them down because you think only you know best. Encourage help, and supervise where necessary. Aim to be the manager of your wedding – not the dogsbody!

Build in some time for yourself

A little 'me-time' is vital to any stress-management programme. Every evening, make sure you take time out just to relax and unwind. If it's hard to find peace at home, go for a walk or to the cinema. Why not book yourself in for a massage? Better still, in the weeks before your ceremony, plan a weekend away with mates to pamper and unwind. Ban all wedding talk (and see how long you can stick to that!).

Talk to yourself nicely

Bombarding yourself with unhelpful thoughts, such as 'It's all going to go wrong!' or 'I'll look a right state on the day!', can make the job of preparing doubly hard. Repeat an affirmation to yourself – a potent, positive sentence that you repeat until the thought sticks. Try something like 'Every day, I'm getting closer to the wedding I want.' Say it over and over – in a traffic jam, on the train – and write it over and over, too.

Just say no!

Now is not the time to be a people-pleaser. There may be people around you who want to have a say in how you should arrange your wedding. But this is your day, and while you will want to accommodate others' views, much stress can be avoided if you clearly assert your wishes and plans whenever possible, and don't encourage suggestions that you know will eventually be turned down. Being honest is the best policy all round.

WHAT HAPPENS ON THE DAY?

In the morning

It will be hectic, so plan your routine carefully in advance.

It is wise to have your make-up and hair finished at least an hour before you leave for the ceremony. This will give you time to dress calmly and pose for pre-ceremony photographs.

Final preparation

Make sure that your going-away outfit and honeymoon luggage are packed and that someone is taking them to the reception venue.

You and your father usually travel to the ceremony together, while everyone else gets there before you. Leave enough time to arrive promptly for the ceremony – then if you choose to, you can observe the tradition of being a little late, without the panic of actually being so!

During the ceremony

If it is a church wedding, you enter on your father's right arm (or on the arm of whoever is giving you away) and walk down the aisle followed by your attendants. Tradition has your face covered with a veil, but few women observe that these days.

The big entrance

As you arrive looking gorgeous at the front of the pews, the groom will move to your right side and your father will drop back very slightly behind you. You should then hand your bouquet to your chief bridesmaid, who will lift your veil if need be.

Husband and wife

Once you've been proclaimed husband and wife, you both lead the attendants and parents into the vestry for the signing of the register, followed by a triumphant procession out of the church.

Old traditions

Once upon a time, the bride and groom would arrange for a chimneysweep to meet them at the church doors as they left the ceremony because it was supposed to bring good luck to the marriage!

Civil ceremonies

Much the same procedure is followed
in a register office, but usually with far
less ceremony. However, civil weddings
taking place in approved premises such
as castles or stately homes will often
involve just as much pomp and
circumstance, if not more!

At the reception

At the reception, you should welcome your guests and receive everyone's best wishes and congratulations. If you have a formal receiving line, you are the third couple in line, after your parents and the groom's parents.

Top table

If there is a formal top table, your place
is on the left of your groom.
There is no reason why you shouldn't
make a short speech if you want to, giving
your thanks to your husband, parents,
family and friends.

The bride's speech

As the bride, you have the most interesting role of all when it comes to the speeches. The other main speakers – father of the bride, best man and so on – have speaking roles with huge traditions attached to them (father dotes on daughter, best man humiliates groom, etc). However, if you wish to make a speech, there will be no such expectations upon you.

When to speak

If your father is not present, then you
may want to speak first, in the traditional
father-of-the-bride slot. Some couples opt
to stand up and speak together (in many
ways, a very logical choice); others prefer
to speak separately and address different
themes (the other's family, for instance).
Or you may prefer to speak
after – or before – your husband,
or even after the best man, as
the very last speaker.

What to say

Here are some ideas to get you started:

- Thank all the guests for coming, especially long-lost friends and people who've travelled a long way.
- Thank the people who've supported you through the stress of preparing for the wedding.
- A special word about your mum, not just to thank her for her role in the wedding preparations, but also to describe your relationship with her over the years.

What to say

- Thank guests for all their gifts (if the groom hasn't already).
- It may make more sense, for you to thank the bridesmaids, too (rather than the groom).
- A popular American innovation is for the bride to finish with a toast to the guests.

The first dance

After the toasts, speeches and cutting of
the cake, you and your husband should lead
the dancing, if there is any. This is known
as the 'first dance', and couples tend to
choose their favourite song for this. Some
couples like to learn to waltz (or jive or
tango!) specially for this moment.

Going away

If you are formally 'going away' after your reception, it is customary to change into a going-away outfit, helped by your chief bridesmaid. Parents usually say their private goodbyes at this point. If you intend to party until the bitter end, do let your guests know, as some of the older ones may well be wilting as they wait politely for you to leave!

The send-off

You and your husband then rejoin your guests for a traditional send-off. This is another opportunity for the confetti to come out, if the venue allows! Your final farewell gesture might be to toss your bouquet into the crowd: whoever catches the flowers is said to be the next to get married. Point them in the direction of confetti.co.uk!

Making the most of your honeymoon

All those months of preparation have finally reached their wonderful conclusion. You are husband and wife, you've celebrated with all your friends and relations at the reception, and now you've got the honeymoon to look forward to. Your wedding day has come to an end, so what happens next?

Your first night together

The honeymoon begins as soon as you leave the reception, and you should spend some time in the preparations finding a first-night venue. If your reception is in a hotel, a night in the 'bridal suite' may be part of the package. This is convenient and saves on costs, but may lack privacy – especially if your in-laws are in the next room! Never assume a room has been reserved for you – the larger hotels may be hosting more than one wedding. Always get room bookings confirmed in writing.

Don't forget...

If you book into a luxurious hotel nearby, make sure that the booking is pre-paid, so you don't have to check in and out, and that you pre-book a driver to take you there. Make sure that the hotel knows what time you will arrive, and ideally get someone to drop off your luggage earlier in the day. You'll need an overnight case, plus your holiday luggage if you're jetting off next day. Remember to arrange for someone to collect your wedding dress/suit the next day and return anything that's hired.

Time for friends and family

Lots of couples recommend leaving it a day or two after the wedding before setting off on honeymoon. Some friends and relatives may have travelled a long way to be with you on your big day, but you may not have had a chance to talk to them. Perhaps you could arrange to meet up with some of the guests for lunch the next day.

Adjusting to married life
Newlyweds often say that it takes days to
really take in all the things that happen on
your wedding day. You may want to consider
delaying your honeymoon until you're
ready to focus on it.

What if we argue?

On honeymoon you are suddenly thrown into each other's company 24 hours a day. You've just been through one of the most stressful experiences of your life (yes, good things can be stressful, too), so you may end up having the odd row. But that's life. Don't think that because this is meant to be the happiest time of your life, that one day when you feel merely content, rather than delirious it is all your husband's fault. Keep a sense of proportion – and, above all, a sense of humour.

Handle your expectations

If you've been living together for several years before marrying, you've probably been away together loads of times, so it might be unrealistic to expect a completely new experience.

After the honeymoon

Finally, prepare for the aftermath. You could be relieved that all the excitement and stress is over, and be ready to return to a more sedate pace of life. But you might find life a little flat or anticlimactic. Plan in advance to avoid this, maybe with a post-wedding party for all the people you couldn't invite. At the very least, you'll have some brilliant memories to look back on.

Thank-you letters

Letters of thanks should be prompt, personal and thoughtful. They may be written by either the bride or the groom, the usual arrangement being that whoever is closer to the giver should reply. If you have been given cash gifts, it's polite to indicate to the giver how you plan to use the money.

The name game

Women do not automatically have to take their husband's surname – in fact, a man can take his wife's name if he wishes.

Paperwork

If you do choose to change your name, either to that of your husband or to add your name to his to make a double-barrelled name, you will need to send a copy of your marriage certificate to the relevant official bodies to ask them to change their records and issue you with new documents.

Final words of wisdom

Remember why you're getting married.
A wedding is a public celebration of a
couple's commitment to one another.
Don't be like the bride who was so caught
up in her wedding plans that she was
momentarily surprised to see her fiancé
standing at the altar.

Keep calm

Don't sweat the small stuff. Every
bride who lies awake for months on end,
panicking that her toenail polish might not
be perfect, often reports back that she
didn't even notice things like the cake
being pink instead of blue, or the
DJ forgetting to play 'YMCA'.

Relax!

Enjoy the day! Again, every bride and most grooms say the whole day – even 12-hour-plus marathon events – went in a blur. Don't panic about whether you've said hello to Great Aunt Ada or danced with Uncle George. Just relax and enjoy yourself!

Keep things in perspective

Take a moment for the two of you. In all
the hustle and bustle of greeting guests,
making speeches, cutting the cake and having
a first dance, don't forget to just check in
with each other and share a quiet moment
on your first day as husband and wife.

ABOUT CONFETTI.CO.UK

Confetti.co.uk is the UK's leading wedding and special occasion website, helping more than 400,000 brides, grooms and guests every month.

To find out more or to order your confetti party brochure or wedding and party stationery brochure,

visit: www.confetti.co.uk

email: info@confetti.co.uk

call: 0870 840 6060

visit Confetti at: 80 Tottenham Court Road, London or at The Light, Leeds LS1 8TL

Some of the other books in this series: *The Groom's Wedding; The Bridesmaid's Wedding; Your Daughter's Wedding; Wedding Dresses* and *Wedding Planner*.